JOHN CARSON LESTER JR

MLM IGNORANCE TRAP

PureHeartsInternational.com
Do Well By Doing Good

Copyright © 2018 by John Carson Lester Jr

All rights reserved. No part of this publication may be reproduced, stored or transmitted in any form or by any means, electronic, mechanical, photocopying, recording, scanning, or otherwise without written permission from the publisher. It is illegal to copy this book, post it to a website, or distribute it by any other means without permission.

John Carson Lester Jr asserts the moral right to be identified as the author of this work.

John Carson Lester Jr has no responsibility for the persistence or accuracy of URLs for external or third-party Internet Websites referred to in this publication and does not guarantee that any content on such Websites is, or will remain, accurate or appropriate.

Designations used by companies to distinguish their products are often claimed as trademarks. All brand names and product names used in this book and on its cover are trade names, service marks, trademarks and registered trademarks of their respective owners. The publishers and the book are not associated with any product or vendor mentioned in this book. None of the companies referenced within the book have endorsed the book.

First edition

This book was professionally typeset on Reedsy. Find out more at reedsy.com

For the "little guy" and "little gal" in the network marketing industry, people I understand and still relate to today despite my decades of substantial achievement in the industry.

"People are not interested in your product or your business; they are interested in solving their own problems." -John Carson Lester Jr

Contents

Foreword	iii
Preface	iv
Acknowledgement	v
Introduction	1
Why Is CONSTANTCASHCOLLECTION AKA MYFORBIDDENLEADS.COM So...	3
Why? Because BIG HITTERS' LIES Have Created The...	5
Why FORBIDDEN? Because BIG HITTERS Have TRIED To Keep These...	7
BOTTOMLINE! We ARE what we ARE!	9
MOST People Are NOT Cut Out To OWN Their OWN Business. MOST...	11
FORTUNATELY, Discipline is BUILT INSIDE of...	12
Most People Know The PRICE Of EVERYTHING, But The VALUE of...	14
Most MLMers Market To Everyone On The Planet EXCEPT MLMers!	16
The MLM Merry-Go-Round Of Ignorance	18
Friends, Family And Opportunity Seekers	21
Opportunity Seekers Vs Opportunity Buyers!	23
Co-Registration Services	25
In Fact, The Vast, Vast Majority Of "Opportunity Seeker"...	27
They CAN. And So They DO.	29

Bet On The SURE Thing; Namely, Hitting Your Target Market Of...	30
Who Wants To Look For A Needle In A Haystack When, With...	32
Opportunity Seekers Come In Only TWO Types!	34
They CanNOT REPRODUCE!	36
Like Shooting Fish In A Barrell!	38
Stillborn Babies!	40
Kindling Wood!	41
SUMMARY	43
P.S.	48

Foreword

"John Lester's Pied Piper Principles are good. I have known John since the early days of Internet Marketing. In fact, he helped me fight off MLM scam artists on the old AOL MLM Forums. I've subscribed to his newsgroup for years and respect John's marketing wisdom highly. In fact, I have beat him about the head and shoulders to print it in Book format. In fact, I took his CDs and sent the MP3 files to my transcriptionist and am pushing him to get it edited now. WHY? Because it needs to be kept on hand every day as a quick reference on "How To Do Internet Marketing" or any Marketing for that matter. When he gets the book done it will be one of the few books that I sell on my MLM Consumer Protection website." -Rod Cook aka The MLM WatchDog

Preface

I don't just think, I *know* that every "little guy" and "little gal" in the network marketing industry failing over and over again and jumping from one MLM program to another over and over again ad nauseaum to their own great frustration and oftentimes destruction would be able to create success for themselves in any MLM they do as soon as they thoroughly read, comprehend and incorporate the rock-solid and time-proven principles and skills found in my 5 MLM works in this exact order: 1) THE BEST OF THE BEST; 2) PIED PIPER PRINCIPLES; 3) the MLM SCREEN PASS TACTIC; 4) the SELF-EMPLOYMENT 101 SERIES; and, finally 5) the MLM IGNORANCE TRAP.

Acknowledgement

As always, I'm both deeply inspired and indebted by the love and for the support I've received in the writing of the MLM IGNORANCE TRAP by the three special women in my life; my fiance Lynlyn Balberde, my sister Jennifer Ann Lester and my mother Armina Virginia Lester; and my late dad, John Carson Lester Sr.

1

Introduction

Hi, Friend. John Carson Lester Jr here. You know, your friendly neighborhood Mentor to the Online Marketing Gurus who in the mid-1990s taught the likes of Jonathan Mizel and Marlon Sanders how to online market (click your "Testimonials - ALL" link at MyForbiddenLeads.com). Your one of only three IRS-registered Founding Members of your Distributor Rights Association. Your DRA Executive Director of Communications. Your DRA Executive Director of Media and Publicity. Owner of the world's only full service MLM genealogy lead list service bureau and full service marketing consulting firm. Your owner of the world's largest full service bulk email company focusing on MLM genealogy lead lists since 1996. Your publisher of not only your MLM IGNORANCE TRAP, but also your THE BEST OF THE BEST, your PIED PIPER PRINCPLES, your MLM SCREEN PASS TACTIC and your SELF EMPLOYMENT 101 SERIES and your Amazon Kindle eBooks and Amazon Paperback books. Your May 2005 New Kid on the Block Network Marketing Business Journal Company. Featured in WIRED. Your $80,000+ in a single month earner. Your transactor w/over 100,000+ people in over 100+

countries around the world. Your 947+ pages of testimonials generator. Your gentleman and a scholar...yatta, yatta, yatta, etc. :)

2

Why Is CONSTANTCASHCOLLECTION AKA MYFORBIDDENLEADS.COM So Special?!

<u>Why is ConstantCashCollection aka MyForbiddenLeads SO SPECIAL?!</u>

Dear Friend,

I am going to say this once and only once.

There is only one correct way to build a MLM business.

Here it is.

In 4 K.I.S.S. steps.

Step 1. **Only** recruit and sponsor MLM distributors. Do **NOT** recruit and sponsor your family, friends and Opportunity Seekers. **To** *find MLM distributors to recruit and sponsor, use MyForbidden-Leads.com.* *(Do you get it?)*

*Step 2. Tell **every** MLM distributor you sponsor to **ONLY** recruit other MLM distributors using MyForbiddenLeads.com. (Do you get it?)*

*Step 3. You **MUST** continually distribute MyForbiddenLeads.com to your ever-expanding downline. (Do you get it?)*

Step 4. Keep your downline focused and productive with the continual pre-promotion and post-promotion of impending events. (Do you get it?)

3

Why? Because BIG HITTERS' LIES Have Created The Merry-Go-Round-Of-MLM-Ignorance!

*In a big hitter's recent book, the author listed the following ways he recommended that **you** build **your** MLM business:*

Ad specialties, audiotape pass outs, small booklets, barter/trade, billboards, bird dogs (referral rewards), brochure pass outs, bumper stickers, magnetic signs, buttons, desk calendars, card decks, catalog pass outs, cause marketing, celebrity endorsements, compact disks, phone book cold calling, contests, co-op advertising, cross promotions, direct mail, discount coupons, embroidered logos, entertainment books, flyers, free lunch, fundraisers, infomercials, joint ventures, kiosks, letterhead, licensing, networking clubs, newsletters, 900 numbers, phone-on- hold messages, point of purchase displays, postcards, press releases, print ads, public relations, radio commercials, radio talk shows (you as radio guest), radio talk show (your own), references in a book, referrals, restaurant placemats, rubber stamps, samples, seminars, speeches, stickers, stuffers, swap meets, t-shirts, tie ins, trade shows, county fairs, TV commercials, TV talk shows (you as guest), TV talk shows (your own), videotapes, voice mail, welcome wagon and yellow pages.

*Know what, friend? When it came time to build **his** MLM business, **he** built **his** current 40,000+ distributor downline (as well as **his** previous 2 large downlines) using, you guessed it, **MLM distributor/genealogy downline reports**! See, **he** knew that all of the ways in italics above that **he** listed in **his** book were "ways" to build a MLM business. Highly INeffective, INefficient ways! And **he** knew that, by far, the most effective, most efficient way to build a MLM business was thru the use of **MLM distributor/genealogy downline reports**. And, so, that's exactly what **he** did. In other words, "Do as I say; not as I do. And let me put you, my competitor, on the Merry Go Round of MLM Ignorance..."*

4

Why FORBIDDEN? Because BIG HITTERS Have TRIED To Keep These Leads FROM YOU And Only For Themselves For Years!

Here's one of our favorite sayings: Life is simple.

When it comes to building a MLM business, there are only 2 types of people in the world to whom you can market: NON-mlmers and MLMers.

Make your choice.

As for us and our house, a house built over 30+ years specializing in the only kind of marketing that actually exists, namely, **targeted** *marketing; we'll choose marketing to MLMers (over NON-mlmers) every time when building a MLM business; for the exact same painfully obvious reasons why a successful toupee salesperson calls on bald folks (as opposed to folks with long, flowing manes of hair). In order to successfully sell toupees to people with full heads of hair,* *not only are you going to have to convince them to dramatically change their physical appearance; you're going to have to also do what clinical psychologists almost uniformly agree is a nearly impossible task; that is, you'll have to convince them to permanently change their behavior! See, toupee salesperson, you're going to have to convince that person to not only shave off all their hair once; you're going to also have to convince them to permanently change their behavior by repetitively shaving off their hair, in order to wear your blasted toupee you somehow managed to sell them, seeing that their hair will have this "nasty habit" of stubbornly growing back over and over and over again!*

Looks like hell is freezing over...

5

BOTTOMLINE! We ARE what we ARE!

We either are bald. Or we have hair.

And we either ARE MLMers. Or we are NOT MLMers.

So wouldn't it just be a lot easier (not to mention actually profitable) to simply target bald people when selling toupees?

Thank you.

And when it comes to marketing your MLM, wouldn't it just be a lot easier (not to mention actually profitable) to simply target MLMers?

Thank you.

Friend, look around the mall next time you're there and notice how few bald people in this world there are. Apart from some little babies and middle-aged and senior men with male pattern baldness and people enduring chemotherapy, most people have hair!

If you're going to be a successful toupee salesperson, you're going to have to take note of that simple, stubborn fact and then target your market accordingly.

And, if you're really observant, and you're able to look beyond the mere physical appearances of people and look into their hearts, minds and souls, you'll notice something else as well as you're scoping out people at the mall.

6

MOST People Are NOT Cut Out To OWN Their OWN Business. MOST People Are ONLY Cut Out To Be Lifetime Employees!

Usually for the exact same reason why most able-bodied people won't stick to an exercise program. Most people are simply undisciplined. And, in order to successfully and profitably own your own business, you simply have to be disciplined. Especially if it's a home-based business; which, contrary to conventional wisdom, is actually the most challenging of all business types to get in and keep in profit.

7

FORTUNATELY, Discipline is BUILT INSIDE of MyForbiddenLeads.com!

See, just like the bald critter is an extremely rare critter, the person who actually wants to go thru the hell of successfully and profitably establishing their own home-based business is an extremely rare **type** of person. It's a whole lot easier (not to mention less painful) to just get a J.O.B. (just over broke) and let somebody else (da Boss) enjoy all the headaches associated with running **their** own business while writing out and signing **your** paycheck each week.

But, for a very few extremely **rare** critters, this J.O.B. thang simply isn't good enough for us. Why? We view that type of arrangement as a form of slavery; an indentured-servitude, if you will. We're psychologically unemployable. And proud of it! We're rebels with a cause (our own time and geographic and financial freedom)! We're disciplined (or determined that we will become disciplined and/or buy discipline thru services like MyForbiddenLeads.com)! And we're willing to endure the pain for the joy that is set before us (again, our own time and geographic and financial freedom and the benefits that such a lifestyle affords us and our loved ones)!

FORTUNATELY, DISCIPLINE IS BUILT INSIDE OF...

Bottomline, we figure, if "it" was easy, everybody would be doing "it" and then we wouldn't be the least bit interested in doing "it," whatever the common "go along to get along" masses are doing! But, because "it" is hard, and because so few people are doing "it," we want to do "it" all the more! Because we know that the rewards, if we persist and succeed, are simply enormous. Astronomical. Beyond our wildest imaginations. Global. Mobile. Biz-Automated. Live and work where we want. When we want. Come and go when and where we please. At any time and at our whim, will and fancy! And with plenty of money to enjoy all our freedom! All Our Dreams Come True!

That's the way we think. But we're extremely rare critters. Few and far between. Just like bald-headed folk are extremely rare critters. And so we're hard to find because, as a percentage of the general population, we're so extremely rare.

But what really makes us so rare is the fact that, while everybody wants the good things (financial and time and geographic freedom) associated with having a Global. Mobile. Biz-Automated; we're one of the extremely rare few that are actually willing to pay the necessary price to get it!

8

Most People Know The PRICE Of EVERYTHING, But The VALUE of NOTHING!

You're likely not one of those people, friend, simply because you've gotten this far. You also most likely know that most MLMers lose money in MLM.

But did you know why?

See, friend, the purpose of capitalism is to ruthlessly destroy businesses that do not bring the highest quality products/services to the customer at the lowest possible prices with the best possible customer service.

And so capitalism has done its job of serving and protecting its one and only client, the customer, when it has ruthlessly destroyed those businesses that do not most efficiently serve the needs of capitalism's one and only client, the customer.

Well, the biggest part of avoiding getting destroyed at the ruthless hands of capitalism is making sure that you're operating efficiently. And the biggest part of operating efficiently is making sure that you are marketing, with laser like focus, only to your target market!

And that is precisely the reason why most MLMers lose money in MLM (and eventually give up once their resources are exhausted)!

9

Most MLMers Market To Everyone On The Planet EXCEPT MLMers!

Most MLMers have been told a lie (putting them on the MLM Merry-Go-Round of Ignorance) encouraging them to recruit friends, family and *"Opportunity Seekers."* Very few of whom, for reasons outlined below, are MLMers (or candidates to ever passionately become MLMers).

And so most MLMers do NOT "hit" or market to their target market.

And so most MLMers are, in effect, trying to sell toupees to people with long, flowing manes of hair!

And so most MLMers end up losing money in MLM (and eventually give up in enormous frustration once their resources are exhausted).

It doesn't have to be this way.

At least not for you.

MOST MLMERS MARKET TO EVERYONE ON THE PLANET EXCEPT MLMERS!

And not for your loved ones.

All you have to do is simply choose to get OFF the MLM Merry-Go-Round of Ignorance.

10

The MLM Merry-Go-Round Of Ignorance

As is patently obvious, to the intelligent person building a MLM business, there are only 2 types of people in the world: MLMers and NON-mlmers.

But both categories can be further broken down into subcategories. MLMers are broken down into MLM Veterans and MLM Rookies.

Non-MLMers are broken down into Friends, Family and **Opportunity Seekers**.

We define MLM Veterans as MLMers who have built MLM businesses that are $10,000 per month (or more) in PROFIT. Not just $10,000 per month or more in revenues; but actual profit (you know, revenues MINUS expenses). We love MLM Veterans immensely. There's only one problem with MLM Veterans. There are so few of them we might as well call them Albino Elephants. Like Albino Elephants, MLM Veterans are extremely, extremely, extremely rare critters. Just like the elephant hunter that hunts only for Albino Elephants, the

MLMer that attempts to recruit only MLM Veterans may go their entire lives without ever bagging one. But that's okay. Most MLM Veterans themselves never recruit many MLM Veterans either for the very same reasons (rarity and difficulty in bagging). We'll explain further below.

*We define MLM Rookies as MLMers who can make a monthly profit of some size; just not $10,000 per month or more (at least not yet). God must love MLM Rookies because He's sure made a whole lot more MLM Rookies than MLM Veterans. And we here at MyForbiddenLeads.com love MLM Rookies too. Why? Because in recruiting MLM Rookies, that's from where **your** "bagged" MLM Veterans will eventually sprout right from underneath **you**. Just like real seed in a garden, you never know which particular seed is going to sprout up from being a MLM Rookie to becoming a MLM Veteran; you only know that, if you have enough such seeds planted, one or more of them, in time, WILL sprout, before your very eyes, into a MLM Veteran. And that will make **you** very, very, very happy, friend.*

*And that's why even MLM Veterans don't count on directly recruiting other MLM Veterans. Recruiting MLM Veterans is a very difficult task. It's hard enough just to find them. And when you do rarely find them, you find that it's awfully hard to "bag" or "bring down" one of those incredibly big and incredibly strong Albino Elephants. The far more productive game plan is to concentrate on recruiting lots of MLM Rookies and watching a few of them organically sprout up into MLM Veterans right underneath **you**.*

Now, don't get us wrong, we have literally thousands and thousands of MLM Veterans in our databases that we provide to our customers. Just don't count on signing MLM Veterans up every day of the week.

But you might just get lucky...after all, it is just a targeted numbers game. And sometimes you DO hit the jackpot!

11

Friends, Family And Opportunity Seekers

*But, instead of focusing on recruiting MLMers, whether they be Veterans, Rookies or both, most MLMers, having been told a big hitter's lie (or having had this lie repeated to them by their upline who were similarly deceived), find themselves on the MLM Merry-Go-Round of Ignorance on a well-greased pathway to extremely painful devastation and gut-wrenching failure as they "focus" on recruiting NON-mlmers also known as friends, family and "**Opportunity Seekers**."*

*Now, this (recruiting friends, family and "**Opportunity Seekers**") IS the path you should take IF you would be the type of toupee salesperson that would attempt to sell toupees to people with long, flowing manes of hair.*

And this is the path you should take IF you're the type of person that enjoys anything masochistic (like pulling out all of your own wisdom teeth slowly, one by one, on a Friday night with a rusty pair of pliers).

We all know what friends and family are. If we're alive, at some point, we've had some family. And, hopefully, we all have friends in the here and now.

12

Opportunity Seekers Vs Opportunity Buyers!

But what are "Opportunity Seekers?"

"Opportunity Seekers," in short, are lifetime employees. Think about that for a minute.

Opportunity Seekers *are a lead SCAM that nearly all MLM "lead" companies around the world for about 10 years now have been imposing upon those poor souls unknowingly going round and round in circles (getting nowhere and sinking fast) on the MLM Merry-Go-Round of Ignorance.*

Now, if you've ever recruited family and friends into your MLM business, you already know why that doesn't work!

'Nuff said! For now, at least.

Here's why, in a nutshell, **why recruiting Opportunity Seekers doesn't work either.**

Opportunity Seekers *are mere **suspects**. Whereas MyForbiddenLeads.com are true **prospects**.*

Opportunity Seekers *are mere **kickers of tires**. Whereas MyForbiddenLeads.com are **bundles of buyers**.*

And here I was a poet and didn't know it!

Opportunity Seeker *leads are laughingly known as so-called "targeted" or "pre-qualified" or "opt-in" leads (these so-called **Opportunity Seeker** "opt-in" leads are actually UNtargeted SPAM and are currently the biggest lead SCAM hitting the Net).*

13

Co-Registration Services

But do you actually know how these so-called "leads" are generated? **Most "Opportunity Seekers" or "targeted" or "pre-qualified" or "opt-in" leads are generated thru co-registration services.** Typically, as much as **one-third of these leads don't even realize that they have "requested" to be on ANY list! Much less YOUR list!** How "targeted" or "pre-qualified" or "opt-in" is that?

Answer: not very.

And for the two-thirds that do realize that they are agreeing to receive some kind of marketing information (but not from you), what is the actual motivation that lures them to the co-registration websites in the first place? Usually some type of a "Publishers Clearing House" or "lotto" or "casino type" come on that usually attracts, you guessed it, **the type of people that are looking for something for nothing**; the proverbial "free lunch" crowd.

Groan.

*That means that not only will very few **"Opportunity Seeker"** leads ever join you in your MLM (unless your MLM is totally FREE to join and never costs these broke **Opportunity Seekers** ANY money); but also the very few that ever do join you will almost always be total **lazy losers that constantly complain** and never do jack squat!*

14

In Fact, The Vast, Vast Majority Of "Opportunity Seeker" Leads Will Actually Think That MLM Is A "Pyramid" Scam!

*Just like most of the untargeted general population thinks MLM is a "pyramid" scam; because, after all, that's exactly where most of the so-called "**Opportunity Seeker**" leads originate! From the untargeted NON-mlmer general population!*

Even many of the very, very few that actually do sign up under you will also believe that MLM is a "pyramid" scam and will be meticulously hunting for the first drop of evidence to justify their cracked-brain beliefs and drop out!

*Kinda sounds like your friends and family now, doesn't it?! Which makes sense, doesn't it, seeing that these so- called "**Opportunity Seeker**" leads are somebody's friends and family too?!*

*And what's an "**Opportunity Seeker**" anyways?! Aren't the tourists* *who play the slots in Las Vegas **Opportunity Seekers**? Aren't the folks that buy lottery tickets each week **Opportunity Seekers**? And just because someone has responded to a direct response ad and maybe answered a few "survey" questions, does that mean that a person is a true "**Opportunity Seeker**?" These basic "survey" questions don't actually qualify the prospect! Basically, everyone in America, at some point or another, has, even if for but a brief moment, and usually on the days that da Boss has ticked them off badly, dreamed of owning and starting their own business. Does that therefore mean that everyone in America is the target market for the sane MLMer? If so, grab your nearest phonebook and start wildly dialing right now! More often than not, as noted above, **Opportunity Seekers** are turned off when they discover you're selling a MLM opportunity. Not just many of them, but most of them, have a negative opinion of MLM. Just like the untargeted general population. Because that's exactly from where "opt-in **Opportunity Seekers**" originate: the **untargeted general population.***

15

They CAN. And So They DO.

*But this certainly doesn't stop unscrupulous MLM list and "**Opportunity Seekers** lead" companies from advertising their leads as "qualified" or "pre-qualified" or "opt-in." You might ask, "Why do MLM lead companies charge up to $4, sometimes even much more, for so-called opportunity seeker leads that are actually untargeted for my marketplace and that therefore stink?!" The very simple answer, friend, is that because of the large number of MLMers riding "blissfully" on the MLM Merry-Go-Round of Ignorance,* <u>**they can**</u>*.* ***And so they do.***

16

Bet On The SURE Thing; Namely, Hitting Your Target Market Of MLMers!

*Save the "luck factor" for when you truly just want to occasionally let loose and have fun and maybe play the slots in Vegas if that floats your boat. Or play PowerBall from time to time just for grins. But don't put your business and your livelihood and your financial future and your loved ones' financial future on one ball on the roulette wheel. You know exactly what's going to happen almost every time. And it's not good. Instead, put the odds against you in this business in your favor by betting on the sure thing; namely, **hitting your target market of MLMers**.*

*So, friend. You're not looking for **Opportunity Seekers**. In fact, we have a **SPECIAL** name for "Opportunity Seekers." Lifetime employees. And lifetime employees do NOT duplicate in MLM even when they do sign up. In MLM, if you do NOT duplicate, YOU FAIL. Looking for **Opportunity Seekers** is about as intelligent as picking up your phonebook and wildly dialing everyone in America, including 93-year-old grandmas who've been happily retired for 28 years. What you're looking for are opportunity **buyers**. And you'll* *find your opportunity buyers amongst your opportunity **finders**. And you'll find your opportunity buyers in MyForbiddenLeads.com because MyForbiddenLeads.com are the people who actually are the opportunity buyers by definition as proven by the fact that they have revealed themselves to be that part of the marketplace who are the entrepreneurial DOers (signer uppers) and who are not just the "talkers" (those lifetime employees that merely answer online survey questions while they're having their monthly reoccurring wannabe daydream of owning their own business on that average day per month when they are temporarily ticked off at da boss).*

17

Who Wants To Look For A Needle In A Haystack When, With MyForbiddenLeads.com, You Can Look For Needles In Piles Of Needles?!

Even in the untargeted general population, however, you'll find, just thru the luck of sheer large numbers, a few people here and there who make good MLM prospects and who will actually sign up with you (and, in extremely rare cases, actually be productive). Only 1 out of 100 "opportunity seeker" leads are true entrepreneurs because 99% of "opportunity seeker leads" are lifetime employees. Whereas MyForbiddenLeads.com are chock FULL of hard core entrepreneurs who LOVE MLM! In fact, you will typically find **30 to 40 times as many true entrepreneurs** in MyForbiddenLeads.com compared to the **99% lifetime employees** in "Opportunity Seeker" lists. **Who wants to look for a needle in a haystack** when, with MyForbidden-Leads.com, **you can look for needles in piles of needles?!**

But, we've discovered, especially with regards to MLM powerline marketing types of programs, that **Opportunity Seekers** do serve one

WHO WANTS TO LOOK FOR A NEEDLE IN A HAYSTACK WHEN, WITH...

useful purpose.

Kindling wood.

That's right...kindling wood.

18

Opportunity Seekers Come In Only TWO Types!

It's like this, friend. **Opportunity Seekers** come in only two types. The 1% or so that just naturally love MLM. And the 99% or so that just naturally hate MLM.

Guess what we call the 1% of **Opportunity Seekers** that love MLM? Answer: living babies. Guess what we call the 99% of **Opportunity Seekers** that hate MLM? Answer: stillborn babies.

Now, friend, you're probably wondering, why on earth does MyForbiddenLeads.com call **Opportunity Seekers,** whether they love or hate MLM, babies? And why on earth does MyForbiddenLeads.com call **Opportunity Seekers** that love MLM "living" babies; and Opportunity Seekers that hate MLM "stillborn" babies?

We'll answer the first question first. All **Opportunity Seekers,** from the point of view of the serious MLMer, are babies. They have little to no experience in MLM.

OPPORTUNITY SEEKERS COME IN ONLY TWO TYPES!

What's the one thing that babies, no matter how genetically gifted or mentally advanced they are compared to the averages, simply cannot do?

19

They CanNOT REPRODUCE!

*And so it is with the 1% of **Opportunity Seekers** that love MLM. Because they are "young" in the business and, in fact, are babies, with little to no experience, just like real babies are years and years away from sexual maturity for reproduction purposes; these 1% of all **Opportunity Seekers** that love MLM are, likewise, literally years away from MLM maturity in terms of MLM recruiting and MLM duplication purposes.*

*You can recruit 100 of the 1% of the **Opportunity Seekers** that love MLM and guess what will happen? You'll end up with nothing more than 100 wholesale product buyers. And only for a time.*

They'll sit there like babies and do what babies do if left alone and not fed. Because they're helpless, after a while, they'll simply die. And they'll never reproduce.

And, even if you feed them, train them, take care of them, change their diapers, love, nurture and care for them in the 365/24/7 manner that babies always require, guess what? They are still YEARS and

THEY CANNOT REPRODUCE!

YEARS away from being able to reproduce, duplicate and become productive in your MLM business and your MLM downline.

20

Like Shooting Fish In A Barrell!

*By the way, if you have any experience in MLM at all, and especially if you're a big hitter and have any kind of MLM reputation established, you can recruit these 1% of opportunity seeker babies like shooting fish in a barrel! Why is that? Well, the answer is very simple. What's common amongst all healthy new-born babies? They have big, wide open eyes! Why is that? Answer: because they are blank slates that have just come into the world and they are rapidly taking in information and gathering knowledge and experience about their world in order to increase their odds of survival! In fact, just like babies are constantly gathering information and experience from multiple sources, most of these 1% of **Opportunity Seekers** that love MLM join multiple MLM programs in order to gather information and experience about MLM from multiple sources! After all, contrary to the urban myths out there, MLM is NOT taught at the Harvard and Stanford Schools of Business! All training comes "on the job" so, for these 1% of **Opportunity Seekers** that love MLM, like they vote in Chicago, joining early and often they must! And they particularly love to join MLMs with big hitter also known as "big brother/big sister" type MLMers who can supply them with* *the advanced training they so desperately need! In other words, these babies desperately need lots of training and they want to get it from YOU (especially if you're established and experienced)! The only problem is, the payoff for YOU is literally years down the road and chances are, you'll make the heavy resources investments but someone else will get most or all of your payoff because, as previously noted, these babies change "parents" (read: sponsors) and MLMs several times (at least) over the years, while they're growing up, before they're ready to even begin reproducing for anybody.*

21

Stillborn Babies!

*Now, the 99% of **Opportunity Seekers** that hate MLM, just like the untargeted general population typically hates or has a negative opinion of MLM, these are stillborn babies. Unless you are Almighty God, and have "resurrection power," you're never going to get anywhere with these people. They not only can't reproduce, as is the case with all babies; these babies, as far as MLM goes, are **dead**! As previously noted, after about the age of 25, clinical psychologists have rightly noted that one adult attempting to externally modify another adult's opinions, attitudes and, most importantly, behaviors, is a daunting and nearly impossible task. In fact, when the pressure to change is coming from external sources, namely, you, most people will stubbornly dig in their heels and cling to their pre-existing opinions, attitudes and behaviors ever more tightly! And it's with this untargeted general population and the 99% of **Opportunity Seekers** that hate MLM that most, nearly all, MLMers spend nearly all of their time approaching with their MLM opportunity. Is it any wonder that the vast, vast majority of MLMers on the MLM Merry-Go-Round of Ignorance are basically destroyed, sooner or later, and, in most cases, much sooner than later?!*

22

Kindling Wood!

Therefore, the 1% of **Opportunity Seekers** *that do love MLM do have one useful purpose for the experienced MLMer, especially in powerline marketing programs.*

As stated before, as kindling wood.

What do we mean?

It's simple. These baby MLMers need something: namely, experience. You need something when you're involved in a powerline marketing type of program: as many signups as you can possibly get.

It's a match made in heaven. They get what they want; and you get what you want.

Once they sign up, however, don't expect them to reproduce. After all, they're babies. They have literally years and years of personal development, knowledge and experience to acquire before they'll *even be ready to reproduce. And, even if you sign up 100 of them, which is extremely easy to do, especially if you're an experienced, established big hitter, understand that **100 times 0 times 0 times 0 is still a big, fat zero.** In other words, you're never going to build a duplicating downline with this 1% of all opportunity seeker leads no matter how much they love MLM. Just let them serve their two-fold purpose in a MLM powerline marketing program. One purpose is to produce wholesale volume. And the second purpose is to provide the quantity of signups, the "kindling wood," if you will, in the "pop!" you've got money/signups email notification nature of powerline marketing systems that gets everyone, even MLM Rookies and MLM Veterans alike, excited (since we all are, after all, merely human)! And fully expect that nearly every one of them will fail. It's the ones that "fail" at their first few attempts at MLM but nevertheless keep on trying who will eventually develop into the MLM Rookies. And the MLM Rookies that keep on keeping on will eventually become those very rare Albino Elephant MLM Veterans. And that's because it is not a cliche and it is absolutely true that you cannot "fail" in MLM; you can only quit. Both "failure" and "success" are equal imposters and equal illusions. In reality, there is only feedback. But that's another lesson for another time.*

23

SUMMARY

And you actually wonder why your marketing for your home-based network marketing business isn't doing better using these kinds of lousy "opportunity seeker" leads?!

Aren't you actually looking for people that **fervently believe in MLM** and who are **actively looking to bring other people into their (and your) MLM business?!**

Instead of meticulously hunting for the first lame excuse to drop out of the so-called "pyramid scam?!"

If these so-called opportunity seeker "leads" were nutrition, you'd be starving!

If these so-called opportunity seeker "leads" were oxygen, you'd be suffocating!

And if these so-called opportunity seeker "leads" were water, you'd be poisoned!

Again, here's why, **in a nutshell, why recruiting Opportunity Seekers doesn't work** any better than recruiting your own friends and family. **Opportunity Seekers** are mere suspects. Whereas MyForbiddenLeads.com are true prospects. **Opportunity Seekers** are kickers of tires. Whereas MyForbiddenLeads.com are bundles of buyers.

And **Opportunity Seekers** are somebody's extremely skeptical friends and family too!

In fact, friends and family "leads" are so bad, we won't insult your intelligence in providing a lengthy explanation of them other than to say that they are almost always <u>*far worse*</u> than horrible **Opportunity Seekers**! 'Nuff said!

So what kind of leads do you want?

You want the kind of leads that we use!

Con$tantCa$hCollection Leads aka MyForbiddenLeads.com!

What are MyForbiddenLeads.com?

First off, the term "forbidden" **doesn't mean that they're illegal or immoral** or anything funky like that.

It simply means that **Big Hitters have tried to keep these leads FROM YOU & only for THEMSELVES for years!**

MyForbiddenLeads.com are people who have <u>**already paid**</u> to join a home-based network marketing program!

SUMMARY

And marketing exclusively to MyForbiddenLeads.com is simply a matter of good old-fashioned common sense.

*For example, if you're selling golf clubs, are you going to sell more golf clubs to people enticed to a co-registration website based on some kind of a "Publishers Clearing House" or "lotto" or "casino" type come on or are you going to sell more golf clubs by obtaining a list of people that have **already paid** for golf clubs?*

*Most of the people enticed to that type of a co-registration site won't even be golfers. They're usually going to just be **someone from the untargeted general public** that just wanted a "free" magazine subscription or some "free" lotto money or a casino "freebie." Very few of them are actually going to be golfers; probably not much more than the percentage of golfers in the general population. Maybe less! Again, you might do just as well, even better maybe, to pick names randomly right out of the phone book rather than using these so-called "opt-in" co- registration type "leads!"*

*But get a list of golfers that have **already paid** for golf clubs and you're going to end up selling a lot more golf clubs to that kind of a list every time.*

*Now that's called **targeted marketing!***

*When you're looking to sell golf clubs, buy a list of people who have **already paid** for golf clubs in the past.*

*And when you're looking for people to pay to join a home-based network marketing program, buy a list of people who have **already paid** to join a home-based network marketing program in the past.*

Because they're the ones most likely to **do it again** in the future! It's just good old-fashioned common sense!

See, life really is simple, isn't it?

Most importantly, MyForbiddenLeads.com have already been sold on and have already bought into the MLM concept. They love MLM! They're true believers! Secondly, they're already MLM potty-trained and know the MLM "jargon!" Thirdly, they have been in the MLM business long enough now that they know other MLM distributors they can recruit and they know how to recruit, at least a little (in other words, they're not babies; they can actually reproduce under **you**)!

Because most MLMers are riding the MLM Merry-Go-Round of Ignorance and are therefore losing money hand over fist, 85% of MLMers will drop the MLM that they are in currently and join your MLM in a heartbeat as soon as they feel that your MLM and you as their sponsor presents them with a better chance to actually make money than the opportunity and the circumstances they are in at that very moment. IF you APPROACH them the RIGHT way! Because most businesses of any kind in America go out of business within 2 years and because the casualty rate is even higher amongst MLM businesses, the MLM industry is in a state of constant transition; and, individual MLMers, battered left and right by this state of constant transition in the MLM industry itself, are themselves in a state of constant transition in their own lives and in their own businesses. In other words, MLMs go out of business so frequently that a very high percentage of MLMers at any given time are looking for a new opportunity to replace the last one that went belly up! And because the MLM industry is in a state of constant transition and because the

SUMMARY

lives of individual MLMers are in a state of constant transition for a large variety of reasons (some relating to the instability inherent in the MLM industry and some relating to, frankly, common personal problems), **MLM distributor/genealogy downline reports** *are like living documents; meaning that you can recruit from them over and over and over again and they keep on giving and giving and giving again and again. When you understand this important fact about the constant transition in the MLM industry itself as well as the constant transition in the lives and businesses of individual MLMers, then you've gone a long ways towards separating yourself from the common masses of MLMers who think that they know MLM but, as proven by the size of their bank accounts (or lack thereof), really do not.*

What would you rather have? *There are companies that sell lousy "opportunity seeker" leads for up to four dollars per lead and sometimes for much, much, much more! People on the MLM Merry-Go-Round of Ignorance buy them every day and they absolutely* **stink**! *"Opportunity seeker" also known as "co-registration" or "opt-in" leads are* **bad by definition!** *MyForbiddenLeads.com, however, due to vastly lower offshore overhead and a vastly superior automated business model, sells vastly MyForbiddenLeads.com services for an* **extremely small fraction of that cost!**

Successful MLMing is NOT a numbers game, contrary to conventional wisdom (conventional marketing wisdom, by the way, is almost ALWAYS wrong)! Rather, it's a **TARGETED** *numbers game!* **It's so simple to succeed in MLM that only smart people can screw it up!** *Your target market is MLMers, NOT NON-mlmers.* **Either you get this or you do not.** *Those who do,* **succeed.** *Those who don't,* **fail. Make your choice.**

24

P.S.

INSIDER JOKES OF BIG HITTERS!

Q: When are you going to start recruiting **Opportunity Seekers**?

A: When the earth stops spinning...

Q: So you're only going to recruit from **MLM distributor/genealogy downline reports**?

A: Is a frog's ass water tight?

Q: What's the difference between smart players and fools and masochists?

A: Smart players recruit from **MLM distributor/genealogy downline reports**. Fools and masochists recruit their friends, family and **Opportunity Seekers**. Which are you?

www.ingramcontent.com/pod-product-compliance
Lightning Source LLC
Chambersburg PA
CBHW030524220526
45463CB00007B/2705